Elephant Seals

Revised Edition

by
Carole & Phil Adams

CENTRAL COAST PRESS

San Luis Obispo, California

A portion of the proceeds from the sale of this book
go to
Friends of the Elephant Seal
Central Coast

CENTRAL COAST PRESS
P.O. Box 3654
San Luis Obispo, California

ISBN: 978-0-9658776-9-5

1st printing 1999, 2nd printing 2001, 3rd printing 2003,
4th printing 2005, 5th printing 2007 6th Printing 2010 7th printing 2013,
8th printing 2015 9th printing 2018 10th printing 2022

Contents

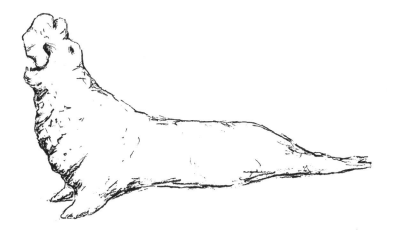

Preface

What are these creatures? Great blubbery males with pendulous noses that give these beasts their name; winsome females whose faces seem to be etched with a permanent smile despite their weary lifestyle; endearing plump babies with huge round eyes, so vulnerable on the beach. They are elephant seals, *Mirounga angustirostris,* true seals, members of the pinniped order, cousins to the sea lion and walrus.

Elephant seals spend most of their lives at sea, coming ashore to give birth, breed, and molt. It is while they are ashore that we are provided with a unique opportunity to observe several important passages in their lives. We honor that opportunity as a rare privilege to observe nature in the wild, a true primordial vision that deserves our utmost respect.

Within these pages, we hope you will find information helpful to getting the most from your visit to the elephant seals. Proceeds from the sale of this book go to Friends of the Elephant Seal, Central Coast.

What is man without the beasts? If all the beasts were gone, man would die from a great loneliness of spirit.   Chief Seattle

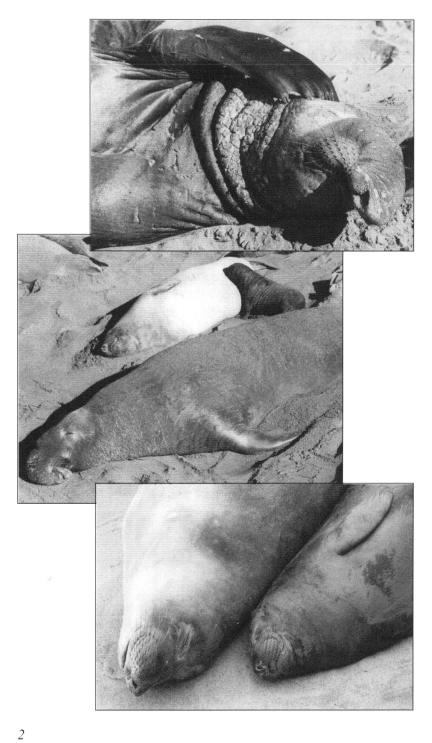

Acknowledgments

The information contained herein comes from a variety of sources, including those listed at the end of this book and from communications with marine biologists, and from the Friends of the Elephant Seal docent training manual. Special thanks go to Brian Hatfield (USGS Wildlife Biologist, now retired) for advice, assistance, and population numbers. Great appreciation also goes to FES docents Stephen Beck and Tim Postiff for their editorial assistance.

A hearty round of applause for the stalwart band of elephant seal docents, the Friends of the Elephant Seal - volunteers at the Piedras Blancas viewing area who are eager to answer your questions and interpret what you see. Foremost, of course, is our thanks to the elephant seals for gracing the beaches with their presence.

Text by Carole and Phil Adams
Photographs by Phil Adams, drawings by Carole Adams

Author's note - Time and further research will undoubtedly change some of our present concepts about elephant seals. Sources sometimes disagree. Statistics vary. In other words, nothing is written in stone; our knowledge of these animals is an ongoing process.

History of the Piedras Blancas Colony

On November 25, 1990 a remarkable event occurred. More than a dozen elephant seals were seen hauled out in a small cove just south of the Piedras Blancas lighthouse. In December the number of elephant seals had increased to over 150. During the spring of 1991, almost 400 seals hauled out and in February of 1992 the first pup was born. In 1993, about 50 pups were born. More and more seals began to call the Piedras Blancas beaches home. The population explosion was well underway. In 1995, about 600 pups were born, and in 1996 the number of pups born soared to almost 1000 as the colony stretched all the way to the beaches that run along the Coast Highway near the lighthouse.

The public couldn't help but notice this incredible phenomenon. The sight is arresting, especially driving south on Highway One. Spread out on the beach, during certain months of the year, are literally hundreds of tons of elephant seals, looking like rocks or driftwood, then one of them moves and the realization strikes that what one is looking at are very large animals. The sight of them on the beach is so out of the ordinary, that the normal human reaction has been to stop and get a better look.

Anyone who drove along this stretch of the coast during 1996 and 1997 knows what a dangerous situation was developing, as vehicles parked illegally, often on the highway, while the occupants scrambled over fencing and made their way over private property to view this prehistoric pageant taking place on the beach. Now, thanks to a highway realignment, and a trade of property between the state and the Hearst Corporation, there is a safe parking area and a legal viewpoint. Volunteers from Friends of the Elephant Seal are usually on duty, enthusiastically answering your questions about this rare glimpse of nature in the wild. During their first year of operation, docents spoke to over 60,000 people.

What you are seeing on the beaches near Piedras Blancas is indeed remarkable, because by the end of the 1880's elephant seals were thought to be extinct, due to harvesting by whalers and sealers for their blubber. The oil obtained from elephant seals was of a quality second only to that of sperm whales. As much as 200 gallons of high quality oil could be obtained from one large adult male elephant seal. The oil was used in lamps for the illumination of homes and streets before electricity, for the lubrication of machinery, and in the manufacture of paint, soap, and candles.

A small colony of elephant seals survived the ravages of the hunts. On Guadalupe Island, off Baja California, a group of between 20 and 100 individuals survived. From that small colony have come all of the northern elephant seals alive today. Protected by the Mexican government in 1922, and later by the United States, they have steadily expanded their range. Today elephant seals are protected from hunting and harassment by the Marine Mammal Protection Act of 1972.

Because all the northern elephant seals alive today came from that one small group that survived the seal hunts, they lack genetic diversity. There is concern that low genetic variability would compromise their resistance to new diseases and make it harder for them to adapt to a changing environment.

As elephant seals rebounded from near-extinction, they first established colonies on the islands offshore Baja California and California. As island sites became crowded they began colonizing mainland beaches. Pupping began on Año Nuevo Island in the early 1960's and in 1975 the first birth on Año Nuevo mainland occurred. It took 18 years for the sum of island and mainland births to reach the 1000 mark. At Piedras Blancas it only took six years to reach that level and the number continued to grow.

From 2013 to 2014 there were more than 5200 pups born on the beaches of Piedras Blancas. Pups are born along a six mile stretch of beach centered along the viewing area. The Piedras Blancas elephant seals rookery has become the largest on the mainland (larger rookeries exist on the Channel Islands).

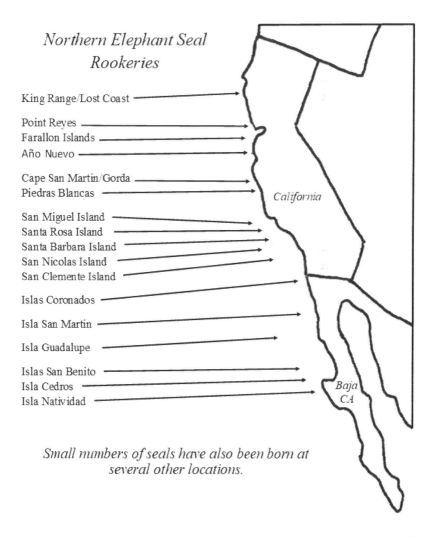

Northern Elephant Seal Rookeries

King Range/Lost Coast
Point Reyes
Farallon Islands
Año Nuevo
Cape San Martin/Gorda
Piedras Blancas
San Miguel Island
Santa Rosa Island
Santa Barbara Island
San Nicolas Island
San Clemente Island
Islas Coronados
Isla San Martin
Isla Guadalupe
Islas San Benito
Isla Cedros
Isla Natividad

California

Baja CA

Small numbers of seals have also been born at several other locations.

Most elephant seals return to beaches where they were born, unless overcrowding or failure to successfully wean a pup prompts them to leave.

Researchers use color coded numbered tags, attached to the rear flippers, to identify individuals. A few of the commonly sighted tags and location of tagging are:

Red - San Nicolas Island   Yellow - San Miguel Island
Green - Año Nuevo   Pink - Farallon Islands/Pt. Reyes
White - Piedras Blancas   Orange - Rehabilitation
Purple - Cape San Martin/Gorda

If you see a tag please report it to one of the docents so the information may be passed along to the appropriate research agency.

Whether there were elephant seals on mainland beaches, or on human inhabited islands, before the sealers decimated their numbers is debatable. The 2020 total population estimate of between 250,000-300,000 may or may not be larger than historic numbers. In earlier years seals on a mainland beach would have been susceptible to attack by bears, wolves, sabertooth cats, and early man. Although the isolation and protection of the islands would have been preferred, it is possible that some elephant seals may have utilized mainland beaches. Because few elephant seal bones have been found in middens, some researchers believe the mainland beaches were not populated historically.

It is difficult to estimate the population of an elephant seal colony since all the individuals are never on the beach at the same time. During the breeding season, most juveniles are not present. The molt takes place during the spring and summer, with different groups coming ashore at different times. Late April and early May is the time when the greatest number of individuals are ashore - weaned pups are still present and the adult females and juveniles of both sexes have started returning to molt.

Researchers suggest the total population may be estimated at 4.4 times the number of births a year. The estimated population total for Piedras Blancas in 2018 was about 26,000.

Historically speaking, man has been the greatest enemy of the elephant seal, driving them to the brink of extinction. Now the number of seals has rebounded, but they still face threats from man. Pollution, disease, and harassment of animals on the beach are a few of the obstacles these great beasts have to cope with. But the biggest challenge may lie ahead, as the number of animals increases and they move on to beaches now claimed for human use. What will happen when beaches used by people for recreation and commerce are inhabited by elephant seals? Can elephant seals and human beings peacefully coexist if they both want to use the same space?

Number of pups born at Piedras Blancas

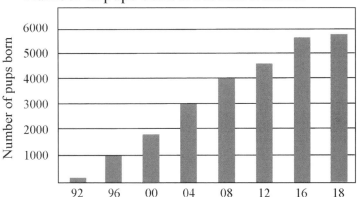

2018 Estimated population total for Piedras Blancas - 26,000. The rate of growth has slowed, and numbers may be stabilizing.

(Approximate numbers provided by B. Hatfield, USGS, pers. comm.)

What is an Elephant Seal?

Try to describe an elephant seal to someone who has never seen one. Favorite descriptions include: a cross between a bean bag and a Volkswagen bug, a lurching waterbed with the face of an elephant, giant slugs, or moving mountains of blubber.

Elephant seals are pinnipeds. The word "pinniped" is derived from the Latin word for "feather- or fin-footed," referring to the flippers. The order, Pinnipedia, includes true seals, eared seals, and walruses. The general term, "seal," is frequently applied to all pinnipeds. Everyone knows what a walrus (Family Odobenidea) looks like, but there can be confusion between eared seals (Family Otariidae) and the earless, or "true" seal (Family Phocidae).

Otariids include the sea lions and fur seals. The members of this family can be distinguished by small, tightly curled, external ear flaps. They have long powerful foreflippers used for swimming. Their rear flippers can be rotated forward, enabling them to lift their bodies and walk using all four flippers. The California sea lion is the animal seen in "seal shows," as they are easy to train and can move about on land very well. In the wild they are often seen gathering together in social groups on rocks and wharves, making loud barking noises. Their faces are rather dog-like, with domed foreheads.

Phocids, known as true seals or earless seals, have no external ears. Their foreflippers are shorter and they cannot rotate their hind flippers, making their movements on land appear more awkward. A common phocid along the California coast is the harbor seal. These shy, spotted, sausage shaped seals like to haul out on rocks. Phocids have a more rounded, cat-shaped face

Pinnipedia

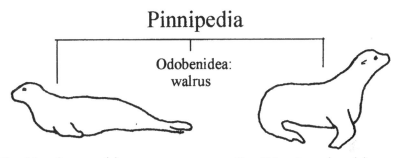

Odobenidea: walrus

Phocidea (true seals): harbor seals, elephant seals

Otariidae (eared seals): fur seals, sea lions

Elephant seals are true seals. They move on land by hitching themselves forward, using their forelippers to raise their bodies, then lunging their hindquarters forward and transferring their weight to the front. This lunge/hitch/humping motion belies the fact that these animals can actually move quite quickly across the sand if they want to - in fact, on soft sand they can move faster for short distances than most humans.

Phocids swim by propelling their bodies in a lateral side-to-side motion, using alternate stokes of their strong rear flippers. With the powerful inward stroke, the rear flipper is spread to full extent, then relaxed on the outward stroke.

Elephant seals are mammals that have evolved extraordinary adaptations enabling them to live both at sea and on land. All seals have torpedo shapes for ease in moving through water. Blubber not only insulates their bodies, but creates a smooth surface that reduces drag in the water. Nothing protrudes from their bodies that doesn't have to. The male penis is internal, emerging during sexual activity. The breasts of the females are flat sacs, lying close to the body. Their sleek, blubbery bodies allow them to move easily through the water, but awkwardly on land.

The body shape and large size of the elephant seal helps conserve warmth and maintain a core temperature of near 100 degrees while diving in water that may be 60 degrees colder. The short limbs are designed to reduce the dissipation of heat. The problem elephant seals have is not in keeping warm, but in keeping cool on land. Flipping sand over their bodies is one way of cooling off.

Elephant seals have 5 digits on each foreflipper, like fingers, with nails, that are present at birth. Almost immediately, the pups start scratching. Most people find the sight of elephant seals scratching themselves to be endearing, because it's so human-like.

Their eyes are big and round, with a large number of rods for seeing in the dark depths of the sea. They can see underwater in the way cats can see at night. Whiskers, or vibrissae, containing ten times the nerve endings found in land animals, are also called into play underwater for locating prey.

Hearing is an important sense and water transmits sound better than air. Their tiny ears holes are closed while diving. Bones in the head carry sound to the inner ear. Elephant seals hear better in water than on land. Even so, mothers and babies bond through sound and smell. The ability to smell is not useful while diving since the nostrils are tightly closed underwater, but it may come in handy on land to help the males determine when the females are in estrus.

The nostrils can close during sleep and have to be snorted open upon awakening, an adaptation that allows them to sleep while diving without the lungs filling with water. A honeycomb structure in the nasal passage, called the turbinate process, acts as a condensation chamber, recycling moisture from the breath and conserving water. It is believed that this process helps recycle moisture when they are fasting - during the breeding season, while molting, or hauling out to rest.

The male nose is a secondary sexual characteristic, like a man's beard, indicating sexual maturity. The extreme size of the nose may be a product of natural selection. Those males with the largest noses are able to intimidate challengers and have better access to breeding opportunities without resorting to energy depleting fights.

Elephant seals on the beach sometimes appear to be suffering from runny eyes. These secretions are normal, and protect the eye from salt and sand.

Besides the male nose, sexual dimorphism is exhibited in elephant seals by the difference in sizes. Adult males are 3-6 times larger than adult females. An incredible sight is watching a male elephant seal raise the anterior half of its body while fighting. That could be a ton of blubber, muscle and teeth, poised to strike.

Flexible back bones allow them to assume some rather improbable positions. Lying on their sides, or on their stomachs, they stretch in ways that would be the envy of any yoga devotee. Do they have tails? Yes. Look closely between the rear flippers to see a little tail stub.

Frequently, the comment is made that elephant seals look prehistoric, and indeed they are. Although there is controversy over some aspects of the evolution of pinnipeds, it is agreed that they descended from a terrestrial carnivore about 20-25 million years ago. Some researchers point to a dog-like ancestor for all pinnipeds. Others believe there was an otter-like ancestor of true seals and a bear-like ancestor of eared seals.

The elephant seals we see are northern elephant seals. They range from Mexican waters to the gulf of Alaska. There is another species, the southern elephant seal, that inhabits the southern hemisphere. The southern elephant seal grows to be larger than his northern cousin, however, the males do not develop as large a nose.

Elephant seals prefer to come ashore on sandy south facing beaches, the next choice being a pebbled beach, and lastly a rocky beach. They appear to be different from other pinnipeds in that they do not seem to react much to the presence of human beings. It must be remembered that they are wild animals, and the time they spend on land is for a definite purpose. To disturb them would be to rob them of valuable energy.

Vital Statistics

At birth, elephant seals weigh between 60-80 pounds and are 3-4 feet long. Male pups tend to weigh a bit more than female pups. In about a month the pups are weaned, having quadrupled their weight to 250-330 pounds. Some pups, who have been successful at milk-stealing will get to be 500-600 pounds. These rotund pups are affectionately referred to as superweaners.

Female elephant seals grow to 9-12 feet long, weighing between 900-1700 pounds. Most females give birth for the first time at about 4 years old, although the range is 2-6. The females do not develop the long proboscis, characteristic of the male. Females stop growing in length at age 6 and are considered physically mature at that time.

Male elephant seals grow to 14-16 feet long and weigh in at 3,000-5,000 pounds, or more. The proboscis starts to grow at age four, as they enter puberty, and can reach the astonishing length of 2 feet.

Although male elephant seals are sexually mature at 5-6 years of age, it isn't until they reach physical maturity, at about age 9, that they are serious contenders during the breeding season. Prime breeding age is 9-13.

Pup mortality varies greatly, depending on the topography of the beach and the density of animals. Since pups aren't proficient swimmers until they are about two months old, those born in areas where there is a large expanse of wide beach, or sand dunes in which to escape pounding surf and high tides, have a better chance of surviving than those confined to narrow beaches with steep cliffs. On most mainland beaches pup mortality is around 10% but during storm-ravaged seasons the death rate can be much higher.

Only about half of the weaned pups who leave the rookery will live to return. Only about 20% of pups born live to age 3. Studies show that a larger pup doesn't necessarily have an advantage in terms of survival. Apparently, the high juvenile death rate at sea is related to the ability to find food and avoid predators.

There are several ways to determine a seal's age. Placing tags on pups is the best method; the tag provides access to information regarding the year of birth. The length of the proboscis on the males is also an indication of age. Another technique is to count the rings in a cross section of a tooth. Dentine is deposited in layers and can be counted like the rings of a tree.

SUMMARY OF VITAL STATISTICS

Pups - 60-80 pounds at birth, 3-4 feet long.
Females grow to be 900-1700 pounds, 9-12 feet long.
Males grow to be 3000-5000 pounds, 14-16 feet long.

Most females give birth for the first time around 4 years of age, although the range is 2-6 years.
Males don't reach breeding status until around 9 years old.

Although a few females have been observed to reach 23 years of age and a few males to reach 14, most die much younger.

The Breeding Season

Undoubtedly, the most exciting time to view the elephant seals is during the breeding season. It is also the noisiest time to visit, as males bellow threat vocalizations, pups squawk to be fed, and females squabble with each other over prime location and pups, and protest unwelcomed approaches from secondary males. There is a veritable cacophony of sounds, including some that are downright amusing, as gargles, grunts, snorts, belches, bleats, whimpers, squeaks, screams, hisses, squeals, and the male trumpeting blend together in an elephant seal symphony of sound.

Toward the end of November the first males begin to arrive and sort out the hierarchy of dominant bulls, the ones best positioned to mate with the most females. Timing is critical. The dominant males will be spending 3 months on the beach, fasting the entire time, fending off the approaches of subdominant males, and mating with as many females as possible. The large bulls will lose up to 18 pounds a day. If they arrive on the beach too soon, they use up valuable energy; if they arrive too late, they may miss out on the best positions. Only 5-10% of the males live to prime breeding age, and not all of those get a chance to breed.

The males are in prime physical shape when they arrive, having bulked up during the preceding months gorging at sea. It is a case of "only the best qualified need apply." Until the age of 8 or 9 they are not big enough to win the battles. By then, they have developed the distinctive chest shield, a thickening of the skin. At 9 years of age they have also developed the long nose, hallmark of a mature male.

Males use physical posturing, vocalizations, and actual combat to determine who will be the dominate males, also called alpha bulls, or beachmasters. Rearing up on their hindquarters, throwing back their heads, showing off the size of their noses, and bellowing threats is enough to intimidate most challengers.

What about that threat vocalization! Originating in the throat, it is a unique sound in the animal world. It has been described as a drumming noise, the putt-putt of an outboard motor, a motorcycle idling in a gymnasium. There is a series of low-pitched sound pulses, loud enough to be heard a mile away. Each adult male produces a unique vocalization that identifies that individual. Males that have interacted with him remember their established dominance ranking and challenge or retreat accordingly.

Size and sound may be enough to discourage some contenders, but not all. When battles do occur, the contestants rear up and slam their bodies at each other, pressing against the chest shield, slashing with their large canine teeth. Although these confrontations can be bloody, they usually do not cause serious injury, and rarely result in death. The chest shields are thick, pinkish, callused areas that begin to develop on sub-adult male seals. Chest shields provide some protection during battles with other males; a bite to the nose being a more painful wound, usually signaling the end of the contest.

Some fights last a few minutes and others up to an hour. The battle ends if one bull is forced into the water or if one gives up and tries to back away submissively. Sometimes the loser is chased by the victor, nipping at his more vulnerable behind. The battles occur throughout the breeding season.

By the time the pregnant females start arriving, during mid-December, the males have sorted out who gets the prime positions. As the females arrive they look the situation over and decide where they want to come ashore. The older, more dominant females usually get the best spots, near the center of the harem where they are more likely to avoid harassment from the secondary males.

On crowded beaches, it may be difficult to tell where one harem ends and the next begins. These are loosely organized units that can change with the tide or as a result of interactions between the animals.

A harem can be as large as a male can control access to. Harems of 25-50 are commonly observed, but much smaller, or larger harems, have also been seen. There are usually beta bulls around the perimeter, tolerated by the alpha bull because they keep the less dominant males away. In return, the beta bulls hope to have access to the females when the alpha bull is occupied. The bulls at the bottom of the pecking order gather outside the breeding beaches and can be seen cruising along the shore, hoping for an opportunity to breed with a female. Occasionally, challengers will attempt to storm the beach and infiltrate a harem. The beta bulls try to keep these interlopers away, though the alpha bull may be called into action.

The alpha bull provides the females of his harem with protection from the amorous pursuits of other males. The females are heavily pregnant when they arrive and must conserve their energy. It can be dangerous for females to be mounted before giving birth.

The females are on the beach for four to five days before giving birth to a single black-coated pup. Birth weight varies between 60-80 pounds, male pups being slightly heavier. Older females tend to have larger pups, they themselves being larger.

The pups are quite thin when they are born, 3-4 feet long. Soft, black, wrinkled coats allow room to grow and absorb the sun's heat until the pup has put on insulating fat. This natal pelage is molted at 4-6 weeks of age and is replaced with a silver coat. By the time they leave for sea, the dorsal hair has turned brown and the ventral hair, pale yellow.

The birth is usually quick, the pup emerging in minutes. The afterbirth is expelled and gulls arrive en masse. The gulls are not only the clean up crew, but the official announcement committee. You can tell when a birth has taken place by the raucous cries of the gulls fighting over the afterbirth.

The mother and pup bond through sound and smell. It is important that the pair not be separated at birth; if imprinting does not occur, the pup will starve because the mother won't recognize it. The pup usually finds its mother's nipple and begins to suckle within the first few hours after birth, thereafter nursing up to four times a day, with prolonged periods of rest in between. Some pups take a day, or two, before nursing for the first time.

Elephant seal milk contains up to 55% fat. Healthy pups quadruple their weight by the time they are weaned, in 26-28 days. At the start of lactation, the fat content is lower and the water content higher. By the end of lactation, the fat content is a whopping 55% fat and has the

consistency of mayonnaise. In comparison, human milk is 2-4% fat, cow's milk is 4%, and whale milk is 40% fat. Elephant seal milk is described as bland and waxy, having no sweetness.

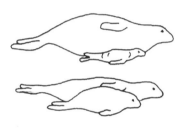

The mother is fasting while she is engaged in this mass transfer of body weight to her pup. She will lose 30-40% of her body mass. Only 40% of the reserves she uses go toward her own maintenance. The rest goes to her pup as milk. It is an intensive drain on her body.

The females nurse for a total of 24-28 days. During the last 2-3 days she is in estrus and ready for mating. This is what the alpha male has been waiting for. His position gives him the best opportunity to mate with the most females. Less than a month after giving birth, she is impregnated again. Around 32 days after arriving at the rookery she leaves, thereby weaning her pup.

Although the earliest females begin arriving in December to give birth, the process continues into February. The greatest number of births are usually in the last half of January, so the most copulations occur in mid-February, around Valentine's Day. Due to the need to conserve energy, there is no protracted courtship ritual; no candle-light dinners in the elephant seal world. The male comes alongside the female, throws his foreflipper over her to hold her down and bites her on the back of the neck. A female may protest using vocalizations, sand-flipping, biting, or wiggling.

As a female leaves the beach to head out to sea again, she must pass the beta and lesser bulls who have hopes of mating. Weakened by loss of weight and the stresses of the past month, she has to make her way through this gauntlet to the safety of the open sea. The alpha bull does not usually escort her. She is on her own. It is during this time that the females are most vulnerable to injury.

Gestation (the time between fertilization and birth) is 11 months, including a period of delayed implantation in which the fertilized egg undergoes several cell divisions, then halts development. This delay allows the female to regain some of her depleted bodily reserves and it synchronizes the timing of birth. Some sources cite a 4 month delay before the blastocyst attaches to the uterine wall, with 7 months of active fetal growth. Others maintain a 2-3 month delay with 8-9 months growth.

A female elephant seal begins to reproduce between 2-6 years of age, most give birth for the first time at 4 years old. From that point on she is either pregnant or nursing. Skipping a year occasionally occurs, especially among young females who do not successfully wean a pup. Females who start to reproduce at an early age also die earlier.

Female weaning success increases with the age of the mother. In one study twice as many older mothers had pups that survived to weaning age. Older mothers are larger and can produce more milk. They are also more dominant and can claim the best locations. Experience also plays a part since mothering skills are learned.

An interesting topic is the matter of foster mothering by some female seals. Although most pups separated from their mothers do not survive, some are adopted by females who have lost their own pups. It is usually the younger, less experienced females who lose pups, and the experience of fostering an abandoned pup may help them learn mothering skills. Another form of fostering behavior is a mother that accepts another pup while she is nursing her own. This is a serious mistake since she cannot produce enough milk to properly nourish more than one pup.

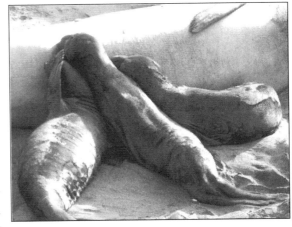

The pupping season extends from about mid-December to mid-February, however by the end of January most females have arrived and given birth. During February, the first females to have given birth leave for sea, while later arriving females are still nursing. The males stay on the beach until all the females have gone. This means that the big alpha males will have spent up to 3 months on the beach, fasting the entire time, before they leave in March. The males lose a third, or more, of their body weight during this rigorous process.

After the mothers have left, the pups are referred to as weaners or weanlings. These plump youngsters remain at the rookery up to 2 1/2 more months, living off their blubber and teaching themselves how to swim and dive. This sounds harsh to some people, but it is the natural way of life for these animals. As weaners, they weigh between 250-330 pounds, having quadrupled their birth weights. During the weaner fast they will lose about 30% of their initial weaning weight. Those pups weaned early in the season experience a longer fast than those weaned later.

Some weaned pups who are successful at stealing milk from other mothers may weigh 500 pounds or more. Superweaners are usually males, probably better at milk thievery because their teeth erupt later and they lose their black coats a little later than the females.

The weaned pups gather together in pods for safety. They tend to move up the beach, away from the boisterous males. With their big round eyes, plump bodies, and silvery coats, they are engaging to human observers. Sleeping most of the time, their bodies are beginning to make the physiological changes that will allow them to adapt to their new lives at sea.

However, they don't sleep all the time. Weaner activities include mock fights in which the male pups butt chests, while female pups argue over space. They may also play with objects, like driftwood and kelp. One researcher, camped overnight on an offshore island while studying the seals, awoke to find a group of weaners playing with his tennis shoe.

About 2 weeks after weaning they begin to enter the water, first playing in the shallows, then venturing further and learning to dive. By 3 1/2 months of age they are ready to make their first trip to sea. The survivors of this early trial return later in the year for the fall haul-out.

SUMMARY OF BREEDING SEASON

Adult males start arriving in late November and battle for dominance. Pregnant females arrive mid-December through January and into February. Giving birth to a single pup, 3-4 ft long and weighing 60-80 pounds, the female nurses for about a month before her abrupt departure. During the last 2-3 days of nursing she comes into estrus and is impregnated. Gestation is 11 months, including a period of delayed implantation.

Females remain on the beach for over a month without eating, providing their pups with extremely rich milk. Adult males fast for 3 months or longer. Although the younger bulls leave the rookery earlier, larger bulls remain until March, after all the females have left. Both males and females lose a third or more of their body weight during the breeding season.

Weaned pups remain on the beach for an additional 8-10 weeks, losing about 30% of their weaned weight while learning to swim and dive on their own. Most weaned pups have left for their first trip to sea by the end of April.

Adaptations

Elephant seals are mammals that have made extraordinary adaptations that allow them to spend most of their lives at sea, diving to incredible depths for food. In fact, they are among the deepest diving marine mammals, descending an average of 1000-2000 feet to forage for food, occasionally diving deeper than 5000 feet, or more. At that depth, mammalian competition for food is limited.

Furthermore, while at sea, elephant seals dive continually, rarely stopping at the surface to rest. How can they do this? How can they withstand the tremendous pressures of the deep for long periods of time? A human being would pass out in 3 minutes without oxygen.

Before elephant seals dive, they exhale. Empty lungs enable them to dive without developing nitrogen narcosis or the bends. Instead of obtaining oxygen from air in their lungs, they get it from their blood. Having almost twice the blood volume of land animals their size, and 50% more red blood cells than humans, they have a tremendous store of oxygen-rich blood.

Elephant seals also carry large amounts of oxygen-storing myoglobin in their muscles. Whale and seal meat appears nearly black when exposed to air because of high concentrations of myoglobin.

As part of the dive reflex, physiological changes occur which reduce the amount of oxygen needed. There is a slowing of the heartbeat from 80-100 beats per minute to less than 30-35 beats per minute (bradycardia) and the flow of blood is diverted to the vital internal organs and brain, away from the extremities.

During the 8-10 week post-weaning fast, the bodies of the pups are making the changes that will enable them to live at sea. As they lose weight, metabolizing blubber, their hemoglobin, blood volume, and myoglobin levels are increasing. The stored oxygen capacity increases 46% and metabolic rate decreases 50%. These changes are key factors in developing the ability to dive deeply. By the end of the 10 week post-weaning period they are spending over half their time in the water. As they learn to swim and dive they are also redistributing mass, changing the fat that initially made them too buoyant to dive, into muscle.

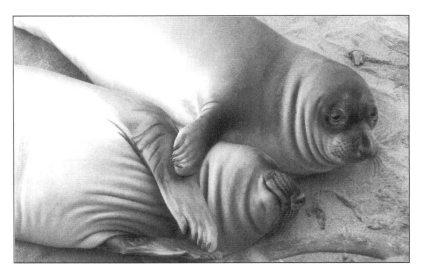

Deep diving ability is not only important in foraging for food, but in avoidance of predators.

By lowering metabolic rates, diverting blood flow to vital organs, and storing oxygen in blood and muscle rather than lungs, elephant seals are able to dive deep and long. Average dives last from 20-30 minutes, some as long as an hour or more, with only 2 to 3 minutes at the surface between dives. This pattern is repeated continually, 24 hours a day.

The shunting of blood toward the internal organs and brain also serves to regulate internal temperatures at the cold depths to which they are diving. This saves precious energy that would otherwise be going toward keeping the animal warm as heat was lost through the skin. With a thick layer of blubber, and the blood diverted away from the skin, the body maintains the proper internal temperature of about 100 degrees, even in cold water.

The blood vessels in the flippers are grouped together in such a way that the arteries and veins help maintain a steady body temperature. In a process referred to as a countercurrent heat exchange, the cooler blood returning to the heart is warmed by the blood heading toward the extremities, further reducing heat loss and maximizing energy. With bodies designed to keep warm in cold water, the problem these animals face is keeping cool on land. While on land the blood is diverted to the skin where it can be cooled. They can also be seen flipping sand over themselves, as a sort of sunscreen. During the warmer times of the day they may move closer to the water. During the spring and summer molt, they may go in and out of the water, an option not available to the large bulls and nursing mothers during the breeding season, who have to rely on sand flipping, or on releasing built up heat through their skin and flippers. By holding a flipper up in the air, warm blood can be cooled.

Another astounding adaptation in elephant seals is the ability to go for long periods without eating. Their time at sea is spent traveling to feeding areas and in foraging, but during the times they come ashore - to molt and breed - they are fasting.

We must distinguish between fasting and starving. To fast means to abstain from food for a certain period. During the two times a year the elephant seals are on land, the thick layer of blubber that insulates them is metabolized to meet energy and water requirements. They rely on stored fat to sustain themselves.

Conservation of energy is an important aspect of time on land. People frequently observe elephant seals on the beach and think they are dead because they aren't breathing. By going into apnea (not breathing) they are conserving energy and water. During apnea the heart rate decreases. The duration of apnea ranges from 8 minutes in weanlings to 25 minutes in adult males. While at sea, elephant seals hold their breath for long periods of time while diving.

These incredible adaptations were not purposeful decisions. Millions of years ago, the ancestors of elephant seals did not sit around and contemplate how to evolve. Rather, through natural selection, those traits and adaptations that proved to be successful were passed along.

Looking at elephant seals, asleep on the beach, some people presume they aren't bothered by our presence. Why can't we go closer? One reason is that anything we humans do to disturb them, robs them of precious energy. When they are on the beach, they are there to carry out important life functions. Their bodies are programmed to rest as much as possible on land. It is fascinating to remember that these animals, gathered together in huge groups, looking so sedentary, are so active and solitary at sea. They truly lead two distinct lives.

SUMMARY OF ADAPTATIONS

Through very specialized adaptations elephant seals are able to dive to depths of 1000 to over 5000 feet for durations of 20-60 minutes or longer. Their blood and muscles carry more oxygen, and they have twice as much blood, as a land animal of the same size. By prioritizing blood to the vital internal organs and brain, elephant seals reduce the amount of oxygen needed, and simultaneously reduce the amount of energy required to maintain body heat. Furthermore, they can reduce their energy requirements by lowering their metabolism and by entering phases of apnea.

Life at Sea

When the female elephant seal leaves the beach after fasting during the breeding season she is a mere shadow of her former self. Having lost over a third of her body weight while giving birth, nursing, and now carrying the beginnings of a new life within her, she devotes the next 2-3 months to continual foraging for food. Using tracking devices attached to individual seals, researchers have been able to trace the route of these animals. In general, the females head far out to sea, in a north to west direction, toward open ocean.

The adult male elephant seal may also have lost a third or more of his body weight during the 3 months of the breeding season that he was hauled out on land. He will spend a longer time at sea than the female, before coming back to molt in the summer. Most males swim directly to favorite feeding areas, mainly along the continental slope from Oregon to the eastern Aleutian Islands.

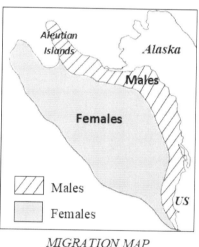

MIGRATION MAP

Adult male elephant seals feed along the continental slope from Oregon to the eastern end of the Aleutian Islands.

Females feed in open ocean. Some overlap male feeding areas.

While at sea, they dive almost continuously, day and night, rarely resting at the surface. The average depth of female dives is 2,000 feet in the day and 1600 feet at night. Male dives average 1,000 feet. However, dives of almost 6,000 feet have been recorded. The average length of dive is around 20 minutes, but they can dive for an hour or longer. In between dives they are only at the surface for 2-3 minutes. They are underwater about 90% of the time. At night females dive less deeply because the food they eat comes closer to the surface.

Elephant seals can occasionally be seen resting offshore in a position called "bottling," in which just their faces and noses are above water and the rest of their bodies are vertical underwater.

Juveniles head north on their first trip to sea, some getting as far as Alaska. By the end of this first journey they are diving to depths of 600-1800 feet, in dives that last from 10-20 minutes. By their fourth trip to sea (age 2) they are accomplished divers following the adult pattern.

Elephant seals have found a unique niche in the sea. At such depths they have little competition for food. Females dive in the open ocean in pursuit of several species of fish and squid while concentrating on lanternfish. Males feast on bottom dwelling prey including skates, small sharks, ratfish, hagfish, and rays along the continental slope. Most adult males swim directly to their feeding areas without eating along the way.

Elephant seals have 30 teeth. Male canines may be 4 to 6 inches long, including the roots, with up to 2 inches extending above the gum. They grab and swallow their food. Most pups have a full set of teeth by the time they are 34 days old.

Elephant seals have an extremely long small intestine, 25 times their body length, as compared to a human's which is 5 times his body length. This great length helps them digest their food quickly, in just 6 hours. Small stones and sand are sometimes found in the stomachs of elephant seals. It is not understood if these things are swallowed on purpose to stave off hunger pangs, or if they are ingested accidentally while eating or spending time on land.

Both sexes dive deep and long. On average, females dive deeper than males, possibly because of where they are feeding. Since males forage along the continental slope, their dives tend to follow the contour of the bottom topography. Females tend to search for prey in open water, further west. The dives of pregnant females in the last trimester are very long in duration, sometimes in excess of an hour; they have to make each trip as productive as possible.

Adult males spend approximately 8 months at sea, roughly 4 months before molting and 4 months after, putting on the thick layers of blubber necessary to see them through the times they are fasting. Females spend about 10 months at sea, 2 months before molting and 8 months afterward, bulking up for the drain on their bodies that occurs during pregnancy and nursing. Juveniles make 2 trips to sea a year, each lasting about 5 months, returning for the spring molt and for a fall haul-out.

Elephant seals live a solitary existence at sea. They usually move through the water at 1 to 3 miles per hour. En route to the feeding grounds, they cover about 60 miles a day, diving as they go. Adult males that feed near the Gulf of Alaska take about a month to reach the area, where they spend two months feeding before their month-long return trip. Females spend about 16 days traveling to the areas where they forage.

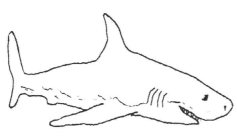

The number one predator of elephant seals is the great white shark. Most shark attacks occur at the surface, so by diving to great depths and spending little time at the surface, elephant seals minimize their exposure to sharks. Great white sharks can be 13-20 feet in length.

Killer whales, or orcas, also prey on elephant seals. It will be interesting to see if there will be more sightings of orcas along the central coast, drawn by the growing number of seals in the area. Orcas are actually a type of dolphin, not a whale. They may reach 25-30 feet in length at maturity.

There is a type of shark called the cookie cutter shark, that lives in deep waters and grows to a size of 12-20 inches. It moves quickly when it attacks, digging into the skin and blubber with sharp teeth set in a circular mouth, and twisting. The resulting bite leaves a tennis ball sized round hole, which does not seriously injure the victim. Sometimes you can observe these small, round bites on the elephant seals as they lie on the beach.

SUMMARY OF LIFE AT SEA

While at sea, elephant seals must put on a thick layer of blubber to see them through the fasting periods. They only spend about 10% of the time at the surface of the water, diving to great depths, where there is little competition for food.

Females head northwest and out to open sea, feeding on fish, squid, and mostly lanternfish. Males forage north and west along the continental shelf, feeding mostly on bottom dwelling fish. Elephant seals lead a solitary life at sea.

Molt

Human beings shed hair and skin continually, barely aware that the replacement process is taking place. In contrast, elephant seals go through what is called a catastrophic molt, in which the entire layer of epidermis with attached hairs and follicles, is sloughed off in one concentrated time-period.

After the breeding season, the female elephant seals head out to sea to regain their depleted energy reserves. Feeding for 2-3 months, they put on weight, and then head back to the beach to molt. When they arrive in April, there are still weaners on the beach, who haven't headed out for their first trip at sea. At the same time, juvenile elephant seals also return to molt, making the beaches crowded. In fact, the total number of animals on the beach is usually highest in late April or early May.

The molt continues through May and into June, as other animals arrive. On the beach you can see seals at all stages of molt, some just starting, while others, who have finished, are ready to leave.

Most subadult males molt in June. The larger males are the last to haul out, in July and August. The males were in competition during the breeding season, keeping a distance from each other and fighting, but during the molt they group together, lying side by side, in heaps, like the females and juveniles do.

Practice sparring among males may be observed during molt, but it is not serious battle, just "working out," getting in shape for what's to come. There are times during the subadult male molt when the beach looks like a young gladiator's camp, with pairs of evenly sized males butting chests.

The molting process takes about 4 weeks per individual elephant seal. During that time the animals are fasting. Molting seals look sad, indeed, as large patches of hair and skin are shed. However, the new epidermal layer is right underneath and the hairs begin growing immediately.

The pieces of molt can come off in small pieces or large sections. The molt varies in color from pale blond on the ventral areas to darker gray or shades of brown on the dorsal areas. Adult males are usually darker brown. The new hair growth is silver or gray. Elephant seal hair is not thick and luxurious, like that of the fur seals, because elephant seals rely on their blubber to keep them warm. They were never hunted for their fur.

Looking at a piece of molt you can see the soft outer hairs attached to the rather thin epidermis. Protruding from the underside are the follicles, which are rather stiff and short, feeling something like Velcro.

Why do elephant seals have to come up on land to molt and why do they have to do it in such an abrupt manner? It has to do with one of those adaptations that enables them to dive in cold, deep water. While diving, their blood is directed to the internal organs, but in order to molt and grow new hair and epidermis, the blood has to circulate to the skin's surface. Hauling out on land, their energy can be directed toward replacing skin and hair cells, without danger of heat loss, which would occur in cold water.

The Laysan monk seal, of Hawaii, is the only other seal that undergoes a catastrophic molt.

SUMMARY OF MOLT

Elephant seals shed their outer layer of skin and hair once a year, in process called a catastrophic molt, which takes about a month. They haul out on land to molt at which time they also fast.

The females and juveniles molt first, during the spring. Since this overlaps the time that the weaners are still on the beach, this is usually the most crowded period at the rookery. During the summer, subadult and adult males molt. The big adult males are the last to go through this process.

While molting, elephant seals frequently lie close together.

Viewing

When is the best time to view these blubbery beauties?

Elephant seals haul out on land twice a year. Looking at a calendar these phases fall within four different time frames, depending on the age and sex of the animal: the birthing and breeding season, female and juvenile molt, male molt, and juvenile haul-out.

Adult males spend 8 months at sea, and 4 months on land. Adult females spend 10 months at sea, 2 on land. Juveniles spend 10 months at sea, 2 on land. They are never all on the beach at the same time. The fewest animals are seen in late summer/early fall, the most during the spring molt.

See calendar on the inside back cover.

Etiquette:

How does one respectfully view these animals?

Park only in designated parking areas.

Most of the time you will be able to safely observe the seals from the bluffs directly above the beach. The Friends of the Elephant Seal docents, identifiable by their blue jackets, are there to answer your questions and help you get the most from your viewing experience.

If you find yourself in a position where you have inadvertently wandered into an area where there are elephant seals, stay a safe and respectful distance away from them. Never cross between them and the water.

If you see seals in the water, move away from the beach, because they won't come ashore if you are there.

This is very important: dogs and seals do not mix. Keep dogs on a leash and off the beach when seals are present.

It is also important to avoid the sand dune areas in the vicinity of the seals. The sand dunes are a fragile environment. People tromping across them weakens the plant structures that hold the sand in place. The dunes could quite literally blow away if abused. There are times when the elephant seals seek protection in the dunes. Let's leave these areas to them.

The most important thing to keep in mind when viewing elephant seals, or any wildlife, is respect. These animals are at home in their world and we should not disturb them. Actually, it is illegal to disturb them. Anything that alters their behavior is defined as harassment and carries a stiff fine.

There is so much that we can gain from viewing wildlife and we are offered a rare opportunity at the beaches of Piedras Blancas. But we must remember, that these are wild animals, and as such they are unpredictable and potentially dangerous; they have teeth, and they can bite. Beyond that, as fellow occupants of this planet, we owe them respect and courtesy as they go about their lives.

If you witness harassment of marine life, call State Park Rangers at 805-927-2068. Be prepared to give the date, time, location, and description of the incident. Never place yourself in danger, but getting the license plate number of the offender or a photograph of the harassment could be valuable evidence.

For a true emergency, in which a human being may be in danger of being injured, call 911.

DO NOT CONFRONT a violator! Let the authorities handle it!

Marine mammals are protected by federal law. It is illegal for unauthorized people to touch or disturb the animals in any way!

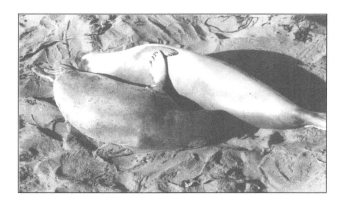

Things to Consider:

Death is a part of life, and although most of the mortality among elephant seals occurs at sea, out of range of our vision, you may witness it as you observe seals on the beach. Pups are sometimes crushed by adult males or injured by aggressive females. If separated from its mother, a pup may starve to death. Some pups are stillborn. During heavy surf, mothers and pups may become separated; the surf may carry the pup out to sea where it will drown because it cannot yet swim. All these events are natural and we should not interfere. Mortality is part of nature's plan. It may be painful to observe, but we must remember that these are wild animals. This is not a zoo or wild animal park. Mother Nature is in control. Non-interference isn't cruel, it is recognition that these animals are wild, living out their lives as part of a grander scheme. There are balancing forces in nature, best left alone by man.

Occasionally marine life comes ashore in areas of human habitation. Sick or injured harbor seals, sea lions, otters, and small elephant seals are rescued by volunteers and nursed back to health, to be returned to the wild. Praiseworthy as such efforts are, it would be more harmful than beneficial, and dangerous, to interfere with the natural course of events in the rookery.

The fact that mortality may be observed, especially during the pupping season, should be considered when bringing children to the area. For some it could be incorporated as a valuable life lesson. For others, it may be too distressing. It is distressing to adults too. Many docents stand on the bluff with tears in their eyes.

Even if mortality is not observed, there are other behaviors that can be troubling, especially during the breeding season. Fighting among males can be quite bloody, females can be aggressive, pups can be injured, and males attempt to mate with females that are not receptive. This is nature in the wild!

Frequently Asked Questions:

1. Is that all they do - just lie there? Why don't they do anything else?

When elephant seals are on land, they are here for a purpose: giving birth, breeding, or molting. Because they are fasting it is important that they conserve energy and not move about any more than is necessary. If you are patient, you may observe them in activities like practice sparring during the molting haul-out, or during the breeding season you may observe fighting, mating attempts, or births. They will move when it is necessary.

2. Why can't I go down there and touch them?

To disturb them would rob them of precious energy. It is also illegal to harass a marine mammal of any kind - violations carry a fine of up to $20,000. Remember, these are wild animals: they have teeth, they carry diseases, and they will bite! Even researchers, who understand these animals, have been seriously injured. Besides all that, it just isn't nice to disturb them. It is also inconsiderate to other visitors who appreciate a natural wildlife viewing experience.

3. Why do they flip sand over themselves?

Sand-flipping is a means of thermoregulation. Simply put, it helps them keep cool. With all that blubber, their problem is overheating on land. It may also just feel good as an activity. A lot of sand-flipping goes on when a female is about to give birth and shortly thereafter. In that case it may be an attempt to relieve discomfort. It can be a sign of agitation. Females also flip sand when trying to avoid unwanted sexual approaches.

4. Why do the males make that noise?

Why do the males make that noise? The vocalization is part of the pattern that establishes dominance among the males. It's a macho thing - an announcement, a challenge, a warning, and like all important activities, it needs to be practiced. Each male's vocalization is unique and is remembered by other males, who may have won or lost in their last encounter.

5. How can you tell a male from a female?

The nose on the male starts to grow as they enter puberty, around four to five years of age. Before that the sex of a seal can be determined by looking at its abdomen. Both males and females have navels, indentations about 2/3 of the way down their bodies. On the males there is a second hole below the navel, where the penis comes out. Both sexes have two nipples, one to either side of the navel, but on the female they are easier to see.

6. Where else can I go to see these animals?

Año Nuevo State Reserve, located about 20 miles north of Santa Cruz. The guided walk takes about 2 1/2 hours and requires walking over 3 miles of uneven terrain. Handicapped access is available by special arrangement on weekends. An entry fee is charged, but is well worth it; visiting Año Nuevo is a wonderful experience. Check internet for current access information.

Elephant seals may also be viewed at Gorda, north of Piedras Blancas, and at Pt. Reyes National Seashore.

7. Is it possible to visit the lighthouse?

The Piedras Blancas Light Station has been in operation since 1875. The site is currently under the auspices of the Bureau of Land Management.

For information on tours of the Piedras Blancas Light Station go to www.piedrasblancas.gov or www.piedrasblancas.org.

8. What else is there to do nearby?

A two-mile trail begins at the end of the paved parking lot just beyond the main seal viewing area. The trail offers scenic coastal, grassland, and mountain views. There are several overlooks from which you can observe sea lions and elephant seals. Keep an eye out for sea otters and whales! This easy, level hike is part of the California Coastal Trail.

9. *Does anyone go down on the beach and help seals that are in trouble?*

This colony is allowed to live according to nature's dictates, free from the interference of man. At times this is painful, because the animals are so easy to observe, and it is human nature to want to help an animal in trouble, but the objective is non-interference and respect for the overall cycle of life in the wild. An exception to the rule of non-interference would be an animal in distress caused by human interference - for example, a seal entangled in a fishing net. Even in that case, only someone specially trained, should approach the animal.

AND answers to questions not so frequently asked:

1. The scientific name for the northern elephant seal, *Mirounga angustirostis*, comes from the Australian aboriginal word for elephant seal, *miouroung,* and from the Latin words for narrow, *angustus,* and *rostrum*, snout.

2. The group that rescues sick and injured marine animals:
   Marine Mammal Center
   1065 Fort Cronkhite
   Sausalito, CA 94965   (415) 289-7325 www.tmmc.org

Other Marine Mammals Seen at Piedras Blancas

SOUTHERN SEA OTTERS. Those lovable, roly-poly, ocean going teddy-bear-like creatures are often seen diving in pursuit of food or wrapped up in kelp to keep from drifting away while they nap. They are easily identifiable because they float around on their backs. A group of otters is referred to as a raft.

Sea otters were nearly hunted to extinction for their luxurious fur coats, which contain from 250,000 to a million hairs per square inch, depending on which part of the fur is examined. Otters have no blubber, so they must rely on their fur to keep them warm. A layer of air is actually trapped between the outer layer of guard hairs and their skin. If the underfur, which remains dry, becomes soiled, cold water can penetrate to the skin and the otter will die of hypothermia, just as a human being would in cold water without a wetsuit. Otters are observed spending a lot of time grooming, which not only cleans the fur, but helps trap air bubbles and spreads natural oils from the skin to aid in repelling water.

Southern sea otters (the subspecies that occur off California) are about four feet long. Most adult females weigh between 40-50 pounds and most adult males weigh between 55-80 pounds. They must eat 20-30% of their body weight every day to maintain their high metabolism. Opportunistic eaters, their favorite foods include crab, mussels, clams, squid, sea urchins, snails, and abalone. The sea otter is one of the few tool-users in the animal kingdom. He places a rock on his chest, and bangs hard-shelled food against the rock to break it open. Listen for the tap-tap-tap while watching otters eat.

Otters maintain an important position in the ecology of the ocean. Sea urchins eat kelp. By keeping the population of sea urchins under control, otters enable the giant kelp forests to thrive, which in turn provide rich habitat for many creatures.

The peak of mating activity occurs in the summer and fall. The male-female bond usually lasts 3-4 days. Sea otters also utilize delayed implantation, though with more variability than the elephant seals. After a 4 to 6 month gestation most pups are born in January-March or from August-October. The males do not help care for the young. Small pups are so buoyant they float like fuzzy corks. The mother spends a lot of time with the small pup on her chest, while resting or swimming, leaving it only to dive for food. Pups begin to dive at around three to four months, and are usually weaned at 6-8 months. The sound of a sea otter pup calling for its mother (or the mother calling for her pup) is a sound you can't miss - shrill and piercing, it is designed to get attention.

Sea otters are protected by the Marine Mammal Protection Act and they are presently classified as "threatened" under the Endangered Species Act. Southern sea otter counts over recent years have been around 3,000. The population of otters along the California coast before the fur hunts is thought to have been about 16,000-20,000. The sea otter's current range in California is from about Año Nuevo in the north to Pt. Conception in the south, and they are believed to be at or near carrying capacity within their current range. To increase significantly in numbers, their range will need to expand. However, in recent years there has been a dramatic increase in mortality due to white shark bites at the ends of the current range, which is likely slowing or preventing range expansion. Males live 10-15 years, females 15-20.

Sea otters in California have something in common with elephant seals; they were once thought to be extinct. However, a small colony survived along the Big Sur coast and from those few individuals, came all of the sea otters we see today along the Central Coast. This means that like the elephant seal, sea otters lack genetic diversity, and may be more susceptible to disease.

For more information on sea otters go to Be Sea Otter Savvy, https://www.seaottersavvy.org/. The Be Sea Otter Savvy motto is "*Respect the Nap!*"

HARBOR SEALS.

These shy, spotted, sausage-shaped, true seals haul out on rocks along the California coast. They are wide-ranged throughout the entire Northern Hemisphere. When approached by humans, they ease into the water, often peering back inquisitively, with just their heads showing above water.

Harbor seals do not migrate. They stay near the coast, diving up to 600 feet in search of food, capable of holding their breath for 20-30 minutes.

Most females give birth to a single pup every spring, weighing 25 pounds and measuring 2-3 feet long. Along the Central Coast the pupping season is around April and May. Newborns can swim and dive almost immediately. Harbor seals are devoted mothers during the month-long nursing period. After the pup is weaned, at a weight of about 50 pounds, the mother abandons it.

The female comes into estrus at the end of lactation. Playful courtship and mating occur in the water. With a gestation of about 10-11 months, including a period of delayed implantation, the cycle is repeated.

Harbor seals live 20-30 years. They are 4-6 feet long and weigh 250-300 pounds. Females are slightly smaller than males.

If you see a harbor seal pup all alone on the beach, it is very important to stay far away from it. Females frequently leave their pups on the beach while they forage for food. They may appear to be abandoned, but they are not. Do not approach the pup, as this may drive the mother away.

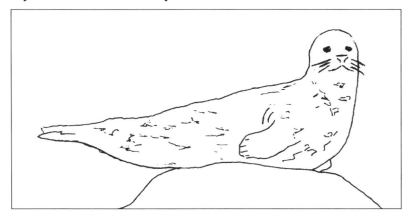

SEA LIONS.

California sea lions are the noisy, gregarious animals usually seen in "seal" shows. They have small ears, back flippers that can rotate forward, and long foreflippers that allow them to move about with agility on land. They frequently clump together in large numbers on rocks or wharves, barking noisily.

Most of the sea lions we see in this area are adult males and juveniles of both sexes. They breed around the Channel Islands and the islands off Baja. The females and young stay in the breeding area. During summer and fall, the males and juveniles travel as far north as Canada in search of food. Once the females are sexually mature, around age 5, they don't travel far from the breeding areas. Sea lions don't venture much beyond 10 miles from shore.

The pups are born in May and June. The mother remains with the pup for 3-4 days, after which she begins to spend time in the water. After returning, she finds her own pup by smell. About ten days after giving birth the female mates again. Sea lions battle for breeding territory, though the battles are largely for show and seldom result in serious injury. The dominant males stay on the beach for two months or so without eating, while breeding and fighting. Pups remain with the mother for a year.

Adult female sea lions weigh from 150-250 pounds and measure 5-6 feet in length. At 7-8 feet long, males weigh from 600-880 pounds, and develop a large bony crest on their head as they mature. Both sexes eat between 15-20 pounds of food a day, making them unpopular with the fishing industry. Their life span is 17-18 years.

Sea lions are intelligent and playful, jumping out of the water like dolphins and body surfing waves. They can swim 18 mph, 8 times the speed of humans, and for short bursts can reach 35 mph. Sometimes they are seen in the water, sleeping together in groups with their flippers in the air, which act as temperature regulators, collecting the warmth of the sun.

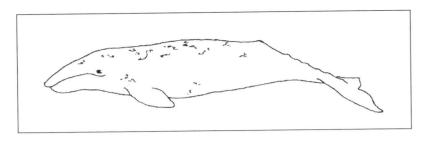

GRAY WHALES.

Commonly called the California gray whale, the "California" part is not really appropriate. These whales travel between the Chukchi Sea, along the coasts of Alaska and Siberia where they feed, and the shallow lagoons of Baja California, where they give birth and mate.

Around the end of November and through December, gray whales pass the Central Coast on their way to Mexican waters. The one ton, 15 foot long babies, are born in January and February, spending several months nursing on rich milk, putting on weight and gaining strength for the trip north.

The adult males and new-impregnated females leave the Baja waters first. The month of March is a good time to watch the parade of gray whales heading north along the Central Coast. The mothers and calves leave the lagoon area last and take a slower pace, following closer to shore, passing the Central Coast in April and May.

During the northbound migration, most of the calves travel on the landward side of their mothers, presumably to protect the calves from killer whales.

Gray whales get to be 40-50 feet long and weigh 30-40 tons. Their blubber can be 6-10 inches thick. It is this blubber that sustains them on their 12,000 mile round trip to and from Alaska.

They are baleen whales, which means that instead of having teeth they have a series of curtain-like plates, hanging down from their upper jaw, that act as a strainer. The only bottom feeding baleen whale, they suck up mouthfuls of sediment containing amphipods (tiny shrimp-like animals) and force the sediment out through the baleen. They have two blowholes and their blows have a heart shaped appearance when viewed in calm air.

If you're lucky, you may see a behavior called breaching, in which the whale shoots it's body three quarters of the way out of the water, twists, and comes crashing back into the water on it's back, sending out a large spray of water.

Another behavior is "spyhopping," in which the head of the animal comes out of the water for several seconds. If viewed closely, you can see the barnacles that live on gray whales.

Female gray whales are larger than the males; they have to be to carry the blubber necessary to sustain themselves and their calves through the long migration and fasting. Females give birth every other year, with a 12-13 month gestation. They migrate at a speed of 3-6 miles per hour, not stopping to rest at night. The life expectancy of a gray whale may be 50 years or more.

Gray whales were almost hunted to extinction twice, first in the 1880s and again between 1924-1946. It is estimated there are about 20,000 gray whales in existence today.

During the time they were hunted by men in small boats, the rage occasionally displayed by these leviathans, especially by mothers attempting to protect their calves, earned them the nickname "devilfish." Today, hunted only by whale watchers, they are perceived as gentle giants, occasionally displaying curiosity and "friendly behavior" toward people.

The Monterey Bay National Marine Sanctuary

The Monterey Bay National Marine Sanctuary is the largest marine sanctuary in the United States. Stretching from the Marin headlands, north of San Francisco, south to Cambria, this is a national park, like Yosemite or Yellowstone, except it's all wet.

This is a protected space, extending along 360 miles of some of the most beautiful coast in the world. It includes 5400 square miles of ocean, going out to the 100 fathom line. With the exception of Monterey Bay, it does not include harbors or bays.

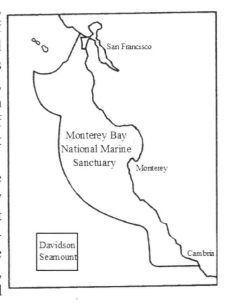

A striking feature of the sanctuary is the Monterey Canyon, one of the deepest and largest submarine canyons on the west coast. The deepest point is 10,663 feet, twice the depth of the Grand Canyon.

Extremely rich in natural resources, the sanctuary is used as the breeding and feeding area of 26 species of marine mammals. An important plant found within the area is the giant kelp, which only grows in 50-60 degree water. The sanctuary also includes over 300 shipwrecks.

The purpose of a marine sanctuary is to preserve a special and beautiful area. Although commercially active, the habitat is protected. Education, research, and recreational uses are encouraged.

Created in 1992, the Monterey Bay Sanctuary is administered by NOAA - National Oceanic and Atmospheric Administration - which in turn falls under the Department of Commerce.

In 2009 The Monterey Bay Sanctuary was expanded to include the Davidson Seamount Management Zone, located about 75 miles west of the southern boundary of the Sanctuary.

If you would like more information on the Monterey Bay National Marine Sanctuary, go to montereybay.noaa.gov.

Be sure to visit the California Coastal Discovery Center at San Simeon Bay. The Discovery Center is a joint venture between Monterey Bay National Marine Sanctuary and California State Parks. It celebrates the connection between land and sea with interactive displays and educational programs. Free admission. For information, call 805-927-6575.

Who manages the elephant seal viewing area?

The Piedras Blancas Elephant Seal Rookery is located on property classified and owned by California State Parks. The parking lot at the site is maintained by Caltrans. Friends of the Elephant Seal, in partnership with California State Parks and Caltrans, provides education and resource protection for the colony. This partnership of California State agencies and Friends of the Elephant Seal, is instrumental in ensuring a first rate visitor experience along with stewardship for the elephant seal rookery.

The Piedras Blancas Elephant Seal rookery is located along a section of the California coast designated as a Marine Protected Area, where fishing or taking of any marine life is prohibited. This Marine Protected Area is administered by California Department of Fish and Wildlife.

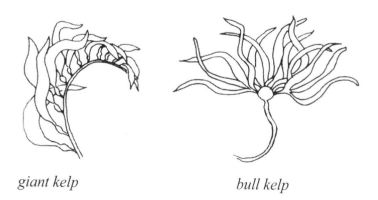

giant kelp   *bull kelp*

Terminology

Alpha males - Those males who have won the right to be the dominant males, situated in the midst of a group of females, therefore having first priority in sexual access.

Apnea - Suspension of breathing while sleeping. Lasting up to 25 minutes, this behavior, while on land, economizes water loss by reducing exhalations and saves energy. Going into apnea while diving also conserves energy.

Bachelor pods or bachelor beaches - Groups of male elephant seals that congregate outside the main breeding beaches. These males may be too young, or too old, to win the battles for dominance.

Beachmaster - Another term for a dominate, alpha bull.

Beta male - The males who almost won. They occupy the periphery of a harem, assisting the alpha males in keeping the more subordinate males away, in return for having the second best access to the females.

Blackcoat - A term used to describe the pups, who are covered with a soft, black coat of hair at birth. Their skin is very loose and wrinkled, with lots of room to grow.

Bottling - Refers to the position of seals resting in the water, with their face above the surface, but the rest of their bodies, vertically submerged.

Bradycardia - A slowing down of the heart rate to as little as one tenth of the normal rate.

Catastrophic molt - The shedding of the outer layer of skin and hair in an abrupt manner.

Cows - Term used to refer to female elephant seals who are involved in the breeding process. Although the males are bulls and the females, cows, the babies are referred to as pups, not calves.

Delayed implantation - The fertilized egg grows to the blastocyst stage, but does not immediately attach to the uterine wall.

Dominance hierarchy - Through aggressive competition, a system of high to low ranking individuals is determined; a pecking order.

Estrus - Sexual receptivity in females; "heat."

Harem - A group of females, usually numbering 20-50, surrounding a dominant male.

Juveniles - Animals that have not yet reached sexual maturity. Females 1-2 (approx.), and males 1-4 (approx.).

Natal pelage - The soft, woolly black coat that covers the pup at birth. It is shed within 4-6 weeks and is replaced with a silver coat.

Sexual dimorphism - Distinct difference in size or appearance between the sexes of an animal.

Subadults - Animals that have reached sexual maturity, but not physical maturity. In other words - teenagers. Males between the ages of 4-7 may be sexually mature, but they are not old enough to win the battles for breeding privileges.

Superweaners - Pups who have stolen milk and reached huge size.

Weaner/weanling - Refers to the weaned pups, left on the beach once the mother has gone.

Weaner pods - Groups of weaned pups who gather together on the beach, like gangs of sleeping kids.

Rear & Trumpet

Sources of Information

If you are interested in learning more about elephant seals, or other marine mammals, here are a few book titles to consider.

Elephant Seals: Pushing the Limits on Land and Sea, by Bernard J. Le Boeuf, Cambridge University Press, 2021.

> Excellent book, very readable and thorough, by a leading expert on elephant seals.

Elephant Seals: Population Ecology, Behavior, and Physiology, by Le Boeuf and Laws, University of California Press, 1994

> This reference book is a compilation of research papers on both northern and southern elephant seals. Scholarly and scientific.

The Pinnipeds: Seals, Sea Lions, and Walruses, by Marianne Riedman, University of California Press, 1990.

> Well-written text-book that is enjoyable to read. An out standing source.

The Sierra Club Handbook of Seals and Sirenians, by Randall R. Reeves, Brent S. Stewart, and Stephen Leatherwood, Sierra Club Books, San Francisco, 1992. Illustrations by Pieter Folkens.

> A handy guide covering 42 marine mammals..

National Audubon Society, Guide to Marine Mammals of the World, by Randall R. Reeves, Brent Stewart, Phillip Clapham, and James Powell, Alfred, A Knofff, 2002. Illustrated by Pieter Folkens.

> Describes 120 species of marine mammals. Beautifully illustrated!

Wild About Otters, by Marianne Riedman, Monterey Bay Aquarium series, 2007.

> The author directed the sea otter research program for the Monterey Bay Aquarium for ten years.

Encyclopedia of Marine Mammals, edited by William F, Perrin, Bernd Wursig, and J,G, Thewissen, Academic Press, originally published in 2002, revised several times.

Organized like an encyclopedia, this big, thick book is easy to use because the topics are listed alphabetically. Over a thousand pages long, with articles by hundreds of contributors, this is an important reference.

There is an abundance of information on the internet about marine mammals. Be sure to check these sites!

elephantseal.org The Friends of the Elephant Seal website provides great information and links to rookery webcams.

www.fisheries.noaa.gov/species-directory/marine-mammals.gov An excellent source of information on marine mammals and more. Have fun looking through this site!

www.montereybayaquarium.org/animals/animals-a-to-z? The Monterey Bay Aquarium listing of animals is impressive. You can get lost all day exploring this site.

www.acs-la.org

www.graywhalescount.org

www.fisheries.noaa.gov/west-coast/science-data/gray-whale-condition-and-calf-production
The above three sites are great places to check on gray whale calf counts.

Friends of the Elephant Seal

A non-profit organization dedicated to educating people about elephant seals and other marine life and to teaching stewardship for this special place called the Central Coast of California.

Friends of the Elephant Seal counts on dedicated volunteer guides to enhance public awareness and respect for the wonders of the natural marine environment. FES relies on grants, memberships and donations. To become a member contact:

Friends of the Elephant Seal
P.O. Box 115
San Simeon, CA 93452
phone: (805) 924-1628
www.elephantseal.org

A Closing Thought

We need another and a wiser and perhaps a more mystical concept of animals. Remote from universal nature, and living by complicated artifice, man in civilization surveys the creatures through the glass of his knowledge and sees thereby a feather magnified and the whole image in distortion. We patronize them for their incompleteness, for their tragic fate of having taken form so far below ourselves. And therein we err, and greatly err. For the animal shall not be measured by man. In a world older and more complex than ours they move finished and complete, gifted with extensions of the senses we have lost or never attained, living by voices we shall never hear. They are not brethren; they are not underlings; they are other nations, caught with ourselves in the net of life and time, fellow prisoners of the splendour and travail of the earth.

Henry Beston - *The Outermost House*

CALENDAR

November - The males begin to arrive, the larger dominant bulls arriving late in the month. Most of the juveniles, who had been present for the fall haul-out, leave.

December - Males continue to arrive and battle for dominance. Pregnant females begin to arrive around the middle of the month. The first births occur before Christmas.

January - The breeding season is in full swing with more births, pups nursing, males attempting to mate. This is a very noisy time at the rookery. By the end of the month, the first females to have arrived at the rookery will have mated, weaned their pups and departed. The peak number of births occurs in the last half of the month.

February - There are still pups nursing. The greatest number of matings occurs near the middle of the month - around Valentine's Day. More females leave as the month goes by.

March - All the pups are weaned, most of the adults are gone, the big males being the last to leave. The weaners are learning how to swim.

April - There are still weaners on the beach, as females and juveniles begin to return to molt. By the end of the month, most of the weaned pups have left.

May - The female and juvenile molt continues.

June - Subadult males molt. A few juveniles may still be around.

July - Subadult and adult males molt.

August - The last of the male molt.

September-November - There is a fall haul-out of elephant seals too young to take part in the breeding and birthing season. The fall haul-out includes young of the year and juveniles of both sexes. Subadult males are frequently seen sparring.